GUNPOWDER, TREASON & PLOT

In 1605, a dozen Catholics (including Guy Fawkes) tried to blow up the Protestant King and Parliament. Their failure to do so is still celebrated each year on 5 November, although some historians now think that the English government cooked up the plot to discredit all English Catholics.

THE WORLD AROUND 1600

*F*our hundred years ago, the world was a very different place. England and Scotland were separate kingdoms with their own royal families. In mainland Europe, bitter religious wars were raging, while the mighty empire

of the Muslim Turks threatened to conquer the whole continent. Meanwhile, intrepid seamen sailed out to make lasting contact with the 'New World' of America and the wealthy empires of the Orient. The everyday lives of European people were very different too. Half the babies born died before their first birthday. Anyone who lived to the age of 40 was thought to be old. Plague and disease were constant dangers, as was famine. Yet out of this turbulent world came one of the finest, most highly-respected and best-loved writers of all time: William Shakespeare.

SPANISH ARMADA

Protestant England was a small and relatively poor European country. In the summer of 1588 it faced its biggest threat since the Norman Conquest of 1066. This time the enemy was Catholic Spain whose King, Philip II, aimed to invade England and make it a part of his expanding worldwide empire. At enormous cost, he sent a great fleet or 'Armada' of 130 ships carrying almost 25,000 men. Aided by stormy weather, the English Navy defeated the Armada, but England remained at war with Spain until 1604.

ORBIS TERRARUM TYPUS DE INTEGRO MULTIS IN LOCIS EMENDATUS

A MAP OF THE WORLD *c.*1600

In Shakespeare's time few English people travelled far inside their own country; fewer still went abroad. But thanks to exploratory voyages by seamen such as Christopher Columbus (1451–1506), Vasco da Gama (*c.*1469–1524) and Ferdinand Magellan (1480–1521), Europeans were now learning that other great land masses lay across the oceans. Yet by 1600 much of this land was uncharted, and no one had even guessed at the existence of Australia.

TRIUMPH OF DEATH

Shortly after William Shakespeare was born in April 1564, the plague struck his home town of Stratford-upon-Avon, killing over 200 of his neighbours. The devastation caused by the plague among other hazards of 16th-century life was famously depicted in this painting from the 1560s, *The Triumph of Death*, by the Dutch artist Pieter Brueghel.

TIMELINE

1476
William Caxton introduces printing to England

1491
Henry VIII is born

1492
Columbus discovers the Americas

1533
Princess Elizabeth is born (later Elizabeth I)

1547
Henry VIII dies. Edward VI comes to the throne

1553
Edward VI dies

Mary I inherits the throne

WILLIAM SHAKESPEARE

William Shakespeare (1564–1616) did not travel the world or have deep funds of knowledge about its history and geography. But he read old books and new pamphlets about the exciting developments overseas. Then, with his brilliant imagination and literary genius, he created a world of his own and gave it undying life.

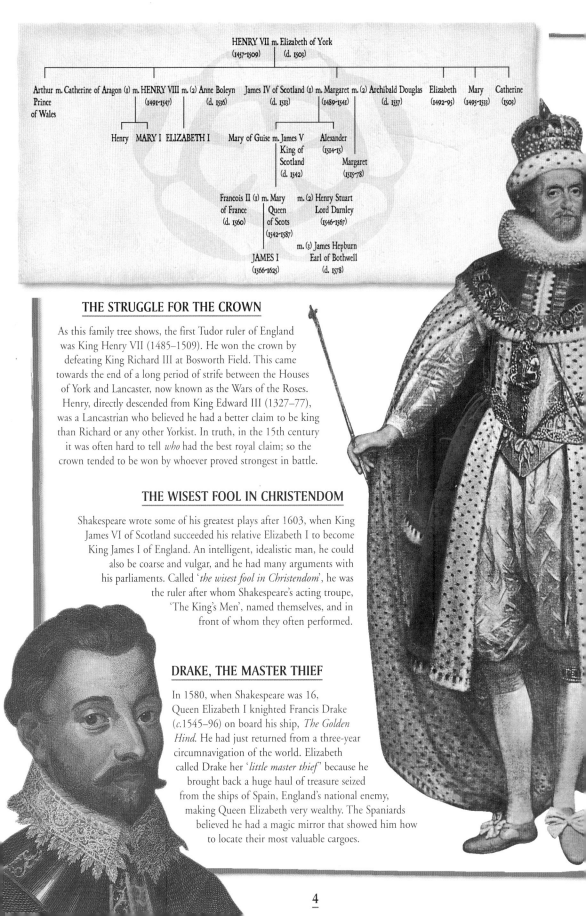

HENRY VII m. Elizabeth of York
(1457–1509) (d. 1503)

Arthur m. Catherine of Aragon (1) m. HENRY VIII m. (2) Anne Boleyn James IV of Scotland (1) m. Margaret m. (2) Archibald Douglas   Elizabeth   Mary   Catherine
Prince   (1491–1547)   (d. 1536)   (d. 1513)   (1489–1541)   (d. 1557)   (1492–95) (1495–1533) (1503)
of Wales

Henry MARY I ELIZABETH I   Mary of Guise m. James V   Alexander
                                                     King of   (1514–15)
                                                     Scotland
                                                     (d. 1542)   Margaret
                                                                      (1515–78)

Francois II (1) m. Mary   m. (2) Henry Stuart
of France   Queen   Lord Darnley
(d. 1560)   of Scots   (1546–1567)
                 (1542–1587)

                             m. (3) James Hepburn
                 JAMES I   Earl of Bothwell
                 (1566–1625)   (d. 1578)

THE STRUGGLE FOR THE CROWN

As this family tree shows, the first Tudor ruler of England
was King Henry VII (1485–1509). He won the crown by
defeating King Richard III at Bosworth Field. This came
towards the end of a long period of strife between the Houses
of York and Lancaster, now known as the Wars of the Roses.
Henry, directly descended from King Edward III (1327–77),
was a Lancastrian who believed he had a better claim to be king
than Richard or any other Yorkist. In truth, in the 15th century
it was often hard to tell *who* had the best royal claim; so the
crown tended to be won by whoever proved strongest in battle.

THE WISEST FOOL IN CHRISTENDOM

Shakespeare wrote some of his greatest plays after 1603, when King
James VI of Scotland succeeded his relative Elizabeth I to become
King James I of England. An intelligent, idealistic man, he could
also be coarse and vulgar, and he had many arguments with
his parliaments. Called '*the wisest fool in Christendom*', he was
the ruler after whom Shakespeare's acting troupe,
'The King's Men', named themselves, and in
front of whom they often performed.

DRAKE, THE MASTER THIEF

In 1580, when Shakespeare was 16,
Queen Elizabeth I knighted Francis Drake
(c.1545–96) on board his ship, *The Golden
Hind*. He had just returned from a three-year
circumnavigation of the world. Elizabeth
called Drake her '*little master thief*' because he
brought back a huge haul of treasure seized
from the ships of Spain, England's national enemy,
making Queen Elizabeth very wealthy. The Spaniards
believed he had a magic mirror that showed him how
to locate their most valuable cargoes.

THE WORLD OF SHAKESPEARE

For the first four decades of Shakespeare's life, England's ruler was Queen Elizabeth I, the daughter of Henry VIII. Elizabeth never set foot outside her kingdom and there is no record that Shakespeare did either. For both of them, their land had special, magical, even holy qualities which set it apart from all other countries. '*This precious stone set in the silver sea,*' was how Shakespeare tenderly described it in his play, *Richard II*. And he was by no means the only patriotic poet or playwright at work in 16th-century England. Foreign observers were not quite so admiring. To many, England was a cold, rough-and-ready place. '*The English have become odious to all nations,*' wrote a Venetian ambassador in 1603. '*They are the disturbers of the whole world.*'

ONE MISTRESS, NO MASTER

Shakespeare's world was a world run by men. Women had very little say, even in the running of their own families. Yet for more than 40 years Queen Elizabeth I (1533–1603) ruled a whole kingdom successfully, so successfully that some suspected her of secretly being a man! Quick-witted, energetic, dazzling and occasionally terrifying, she never married but devoted all her talents to keeping her kingdom at peace and secure from external attack. '*I know I have the body a weak and feeble woman,*' she said in 1588, '*but I have the heart and stomach of a king, and a king of England too.*'

SHAKESPEARE'S COUNTY

Modern road signs tell drivers travelling into Warwickshire that they are now entering 'Shakespeare's County'. This map shows the shire at the start of the 17th century. Shakespeare was born and died in the leafy market town of Stratford-upon-Avon. To the north of the town lay the Forest of Arden, much of which had become cultivated farmland by Shakespeare's time. In his comedy, *As You Like It*, he re-created the ancient forest as a place of banishment and magic.

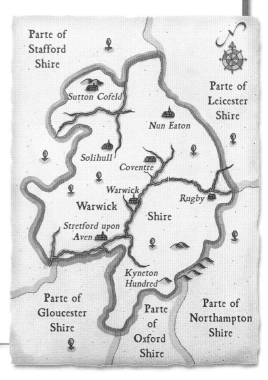

SHAKESPEARE'S CONTEMPORARIES

hakespeare's play-writing career lasted from the early 1590s until his death in 1616. Thirty-eight of his plays have survived, and so have more than 200 others by his fellow dramatists. This was a 'Golden Age' in the history of the English theatre, and its plays are still performed today. But although drama was so popular, many of the men who wrote or performed it were thought to be disreputable. Fine writers like Christopher Marlowe, Thomas Nashe, Ben Jonson and Thomas Kyd all led turbulent lives, and many died in squalid circumstances. One London writer who could not cope with the brilliance of Shakespeare's work was Robert Greene who bitterly attacked him as an 'upstart crow'.

A PRICE OF SIN

This is a scene from *Doctor Faustus*, a dark and thrilling play written around 1590. Its author was Christopher Marlowe (1564–93), a man just two months younger than Shakespeare. The play's hero sells his soul to practise the forbidden arts of magic, but is finally carried off to Hell. Marlowe's other energetic, daring plays included *Tamburlaine*, *The Jew of Malta* and *The Massacre at Paris*.

KYD THE CROWD-PLEASER

One of the most popular plays of Elizabethan times was *The Spanish Tragedy*, from around 1586. A story of revenge, full of bloodthirsty scenes, its author was Thomas Kyd (1557–95). Whereas the heroes of earlier tragedies were usually kings or princes, Kyd's Hieronimo was of lower rank, so audiences felt more able to identify with him. Another of Kyd's plays, now lost, may have influenced Shakespeare when he wrote his own great tragedy, *Hamlet*.

THE

SPANISH TRAGE-
die, Containing the lamentable
end of *Don Horatio*, and *Bel-imperia*:
with the pittifull death of
olde *Hieronimo*.

Newly corrected and amended of such grosse faults as
passed in the first impression.

AT LONDON
Printed by *Edward Allde*, for
Edward White.

SIMPLE DRAMATIST OR SPY?

There is no record of violence in Shakespeare's life, but Ben Jonson killed a man in a duel, and Christopher Marlowe (*left*) died from stab wounds received in a pub fight. Although Marlowe was only 29, he had lived wildly and at the time of his death he was about to be arrested for atheism.

It is thought by some historians that while still at Cambridge University, he served as a spy for the government in mainland Europe and was possibly killed by another spy.

THE MAN BEHIND THE MASQUES

This costume was designed by the architect Inigo Jones (1573–1652), to be worn at James I's court in Ben Jonson's *Masque of Blackness*. Deeply inspired by the art and architecture he found on two visits to Italy, Jones also devised enchanting scenery for court performances. Many of the buildings he designed are standing today, including the Queen's House at Greenwich and the Whitehall Banqueting House.

TIMELINE

1556
John Shakespeare marries Mary Arden

1558
Mary I dies. Elizabeth I is crowned Queen

1564
Shakespeare is born 23 April

He is baptised on 26 April at the Holy Trinity Church in Stratford-Upon-Avon

Christopher Marlowe is born

1572
Ben Jonson is born

1580
Sir Francis Drake circumnavigates the world in the Golden Hind

1582
Shakespeare marries Anne Hathaway

1583
Shakespeare's first child, Susanna, is born

1585
Shakespeare's twins, Hamnet, and Judith born

1586
The Spanish Tragedy is written by Thomas Kyd

BEN JONSON

The poet Ben Jonson (1572–1637) was one of London's most popular playwrights during the reign of James I. Patronized by the King, he created with Inigo Jones a series of masques – elaborate shows featuring music, dancing and drama that were performed at court. His best-loved theatre plays, still staged today, are *Volpone* (1605) and *The Alchemist* (1610). His friend and rival Shakespeare, who acted as well as wrote, appeared in some of Jonson's dramas. But, unlike most of his fellow playwrights, Jonson made sure his plays were printed up and published in his own lifetime, and that he received full credit for them.

LEARNING IN LATIN

'*Then the whining schoolboy, with his satchel, / And shining morning face, creeping like Snail / Unwillingly to school.*' That could have been written in any era, but it comes from Shakespeare's *As You Like It*. It is assumed that Shakespeare attended the local grammar school in Stratford, where he would have learned almost nothing but Latin grammar. There were few books, so long passages had to be learned by heart, and Latin had to be spoken as well as written. With lessons lasting for up to ten hours a day, for six days a week, it is not surprising that school holidays were sometimes called 'remedies'.

ANNE HATHAWAY'S COTTAGE

This is the farmhouse, at Shottery just outside Stratford, where Shakespeare's future wife Anne Hathaway grew up. Still standing today, 'Anne Hathaway's Cottage' (so-called since 1795) is a popular tourist attraction – although with 12 rooms it is bigger than a standard cottage. When Anne lived here, it must have stood almost at the edge of the Forest of Arden.

TIMELINE

c.1587
Shakespeare moves to London

1588
Sir Francis Drake defeats the Spanish Armada

1590
Doctor Faustus is written by Christopher Marlowe

1593
Venus and Adonis is the first of Shakespeare's works to be published

1594
Shakespeare writes and performs for the 'Lord Chamberlain's Men'

The Rape of Lucrece is published

HAND IN GLOVE

John Shakespeare was a glover and curer of soft skins for gloves, like this beautiful pair that dates from the reign of Elizabeth I. He became an important local figure, reaching the position of bailiff and owning several houses. He lived until 1601, but in the latter part of his life his business was less successful and he ceased to perform official duties. Some scholars believe he was a Catholic who suffered discrimination at the hands of the Protestants.

THE EARLY YEARS

Stratford-upon-Avon was a town of about 1,500 people in the 16th century. Crowds of all ages would gather when travelling companies of actors came to perform the latest plays. Shakespeare may have dreamed of joining one, but at 19 he was still in Stratford, with a young family of his own to look after. Shakespeare married Anne Hathaway in 1582 and over the next two years they had three children: first Susanna, then the twins Judith and Hamnet. The surviving records tell us no more about Shakespeare's life for the rest of the 1580s. We cannot even be sure how he made his living, but we do know that no written work of his exists from this period.

FIRST HOME

Shakespeare was born here in Henley Street, and his baptism was recorded on 26 April 1564. It is thought that he was born on 23 April, the feast day of Saint George, England's patron saint. He was the eldest of six children who lived with their parents in a fine half-timbered house like this one.

POSH PARENTS

According to this page from the parish register, 'Gulielmus' (Latin for William) was baptised as 'Gulielmus filius Johannes Shakspere' the son of John Shakespeare. John had married Mary Arden, who came from a wealthy local landowning family, in 1556. Their first two children, both girls, died before Shakespeare was born. Although their family was large, by 16th-century standards they lived in relative luxury.

TRAVELLING BANDS

When Shakespeare was a boy, there were no purpose-built theatres in Stratford or in any other provincial town. Licences were issued to bands of travelling players, who performed in the courtyards of inns or similarly suitable open spaces. Life on the roads of England could be difficult, so any pennies the actors collected were hard-earned.

9

SHAKESPEARE IN LONDON

No one can be sure why or when Shakespeare moved from Stratford to London, but by 1592 he had made a name for himself there as an actor and playwright. The teeming city held ten times as many people as his provincial hometown. Grand buildings like the Tower and Royal Exchange dwarfed the cramped slums of the poor, and although there were warrens of streets and alleys, the city's busiest highway by far was the wide River Thames. From 1594 Shakespeare wrote and acted for just one company, the 'Lord Chamberlain's Men'. It included two 'players' much more famous than him at the time: William Kempe, who excelled in comic roles, and Richard Burbage, the greatest tragic hero of the age. They performed in the new open-air 'playhouses' south of the river. Actresses were not an attraction as the female roles were all played by young men!

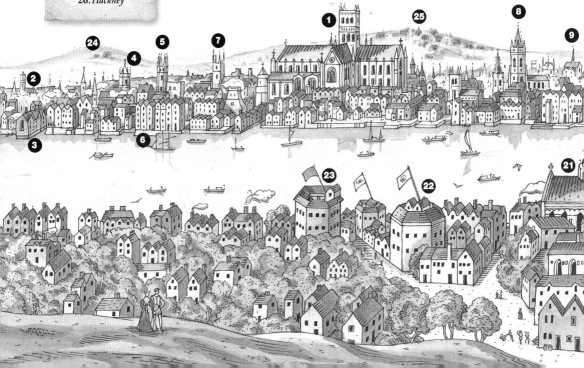

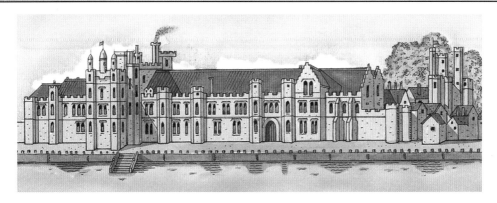

ROYAL COMMAND PERFORMANCES

Farther down river was the royal palace of Greenwich, the birthplace of Queen Elizabeth I. It became the venue for almost 200 royal performances by the 'King's Men', the new name given to the Lord Chamberlain's Men when James I became the company's patron. Shakespeare had to carefully edit out any parts of his plays that incurred the censor's disapproval.

THE GLOBE

The capital's entertainment quarter was to the south of the river in Bankside. The Rose, the Swan and the Hope theatres were all here, where travelling players had once performed. From 1599, the Globe Theatre was a new venue for plays by the Lord Chamberlain's Men. It held audiences of up to 2,500 people and had to be rebuilt after it was burned down during a performance of *Henry VIII* in 1613.

THE BEAR GARDEN

Close to the Globe stood the Bear Garden. People would go to places like this to watch bears forced to fight with savage dogs. Bear baiting and cock fighting were common forms of entertainment at the time.

LIFE ON THE WATER

London Bridge, the only bridge across the Thames, was more like a street than a bridge. Along either side stood rows of closely-built houses. Sometimes when the river froze over, 'Frost Fairs' were held on its surface, with shops, booths, skating and horse-racing.

SYMBOL OF SHAKESPEARE'S SUCCESS

This '*pretty house of brick and timber*' is New Place, the Stratford home that Shakespeare bought in 1597. Built by Sir Hugh Clopton in the 15th century, it was the second-biggest house in Stratford and had no fewer than 10 fireplaces. As a shareholder in his theatrical company, Shakespeare became a rich man, able to afford such luxury.

BRINGING THE BARD TO BOOK

Shakespeare was born far too late to meet William Caxton (*c*.1420–92), shown above in his workshop. But by introducing the art of printing to England around 1476, Caxton made it possible for Shakespeare's works to survive for centuries on the page as well as on the stage. His press brought to an end the long era when all books had to be painstakingly written by hand.

FIRST FOLIO

This is the kind of press on which Shakespeare's plays would have been printed. Few playwrights in his time had their works published, although Shakespeare's first two poems and his *Sonnets* were published while he was still alive. After his death, two of his friends, John Heminges and Richard Condell, gathered up the texts of 36 of his plays and had them published in a 900-page First Folio (1623), with a dedication by Ben Jonson.

THE LAST YEARS

While Shakespeare won immortal fame in London, his wife and young family continued to live two days' ride away in Stratford. Shakespeare must have returned whenever he could, but after August 1596 he had only two children to visit, since his son Hamnet fell ill and died at the age of just 11. In the next year, Shakespeare bought a grand new home and was now officially a 'gentleman', allowed to display a coat of arms showing a falcon and a spear. In his last years he bought more land in Stratford and spent less time in London.

A prolific writer, he had produced work of the highest literary merit, and now he had all the outward trappings of success too. He died on his 52nd birthday – 23 April 1616.

LITERARY LEGACY

Shakespeare was buried in the Holy Trinity Church, Stratford. The last line of his epitaph reads:
'*Curst be he that moves my bones.*'

Since this monument was made during the lifetime of Shakespeare's surviving family, it probably gives a fair impression of what he really looked like in later years.

WILL'S WILL

On 25 March 1616, Shakespeare signed a new will. It provides a rare surviving example of his signature, and of the hand in which he wrote all his poems and plays. He may have revised his will to protect his daughter, Judith, who had recently married. To his wife, Anne, Shakespeare left his '*second-best bed with the furniture*' (i.e. the bed linen and hangings). To this day no one really knows what he meant by this gesture.

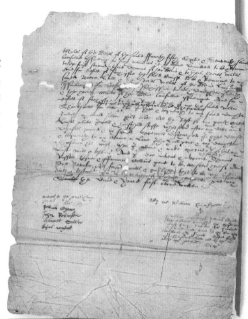

COMEDIES BEFORE 1600

WOMAN IN A MAN'S WORLD

The feisty heroine of *The Merchant of Venice* is Portia, shown here in her Italian garden. Her father gives her in marriage to the suitor who picks the 'right' casket, when presented with a choice of three. But Portia finds herself in a man's world when she disguises herself as a male lawyer and wins a vital court case to save her fiance's life.

*I*n the First Folio of Shakespeare's works, published in 1623, the editors divided the plays into three categories: comedies, histories and tragedies, yet sometimes it is hard to tell in which category a play belongs. *The Merchant of Venice*, for example, has plenty of funny moments, but it also deals with the deadly serious matters of justice and the attitudes of Christians and Jews towards each other. In *Hamlet*, which is both tragic and historical, an old man called Polonius lists the possible types of play as: '*tragedy, comedy, history, pastoral, pastoral-comical, historical-pastoral, tragical-historical, tragical-comical-historical-pastoral.*' Most of Shakespeare's plays mix up the types. But in the 1590s he showed he had a magic touch for writing light, mainly gentle, largely romantic comedies – with plenty of scope for illusion and deception.

COMEDY WITH AN EDGE

The two lovebirds shown here are Benedick and Beatrice, characters in *Much Ado About Nothing*. The play's title is a little misleading, for although there is a lot of light-hearted fun – especially in the banter between Benedick and Beatrice the central story is quite dark. It centres on a soldier tricked by an evil-minded colleague into believing that the woman he loves has been unfaithful to him. Shakespeare used this idea again in his later tragedy *Othello*.

SHAKESPEARE'S SEX WAR

Elizabeth Taylor and Richard Burton are shown here in Franco Zeffirelli's 1967 film version of *The Taming of the Shrew*. The play features an Elizabethan battle of the sexes. Kate, a wilful, 'shrewish' girl, marries Petruchio, who bets that he can wear her down into becoming a gentle, well-behaved wife. He seems to have won his bet when Kate finally declares that; '*Such duty as the subject owes the prince, Even such a woman oweth to her husband.*'

Taylor and Burton were married in real life – twice!

FALSTAFF THE FOOL

The sub-plot of Shakespeare's *Henry IV* features a comic character called Sir John Falstaff. According to legend, he amused Queen Elizabeth I so much that she ordered Shakespeare to write him into another play and show him in love. The result was *The Merry Wives of Windsor* in which Falstaff bungles his attempts to seduce the wives of the title.

LOVE CONQUERS ALL?

This picture shows a scene from a modern adaptation of *Love's Labour's Lost*, the first play to carry Shakespeare's name as author. A favourite play of Queen Elizabeth I, this witty romp focuses on a love affair between the King of Navarre and the daughter of the King of France. There is an unexpected, cliff-hanger ending, for the lovers finally have to part for a year. Maybe they will then get together again, but maybe they will not.

COMEDIES AFTER 1600

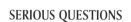

Shakespeare's early comedies were rarely simple. But after his theatrical company moved to the Globe in the late 1590s, his comic writing had an even sharper, sometimes darker edge. Mostly based on existing stories, these new plays are known as his 'mature' comedies, ranging from the identity mix-ups of *Twelfth Night* and the trickery of *All's Well That Ends Well* to the fairytale atmosphere of *The Winter's Tale*. Special effects played a key part in some of them. In one scene in *The Tempest,* a banquet was made to disappear 'magically' – using hidden pulleys and trapdoors. These effects became more stunning when, after 1609, 'The King's Men' took over a small, indoor, private theatre called Blackfriars. The actors could now perform by candlelight at night-time, as well as in the open-air Globe in the afternoons.

SERIOUS QUESTIONS

Measure for Measure, from early in the reign of King James I, is a very dark comedy. In many comedies of the time, the action concludes with a 'happy-ever-after' marriage or two. But Isabella, who is shown here, finally responds to Duke Vincentio's marriage proposal with silence.

WHAT HAPPENS NEXT?

All's Well That Ends Well may be a slightly misleading title. This romantic comedy features Helena, who is deeply in love with Bertram – who is deeply not in love with her. Through tricks and illusions Helena gets her man in the end, but as with many of Shakespeare's plays, the audience is left wondering what the future might hold for the main characters.

16

'NOTHING THAT IS SO, IS SO'

Twelfth Night was performed for the lawyers here at Middle Temple Hall, one of London's 'Inns of Court', on 2 February 1602. The play features one female character, Viola, taking on the identity of a man – mistaken identity being a common feature of Shakespeare's plays. Shakespeare based *Twelfth Night* on several sources, including *Gi 'Ingannati*, an Italian farce in which male and female twins are constantly mistaken for each other.

SHORT & SWEET

The Tempest is Shakespeare's shortest play – no doubt a good thing for King James I, who did not like long entertainments. The play was performed at court in 1613 to celebrate the wedding of James' daughter Princess Elizabeth and the German Prince Frederick of the Palatinate. The picture shows a scene from their marriage festivities, five years before they became the rulers of Bohemia. Their grandson later became King George I of England.

LEONTES' TRUE DAUGHTER

This is Perdita, daughter of Leontes in Shakespeare's late 'tragi-comedy', *The Winter's Tale*. Suspecting that his wife has been unfaithful to him, Leontes dreads that his children are not truly his own. The play seeks to confirm their true identity with Leontes' suspicions being lifted at the end. The play was based on the novel *Pandosto* by Robert Greene.

THE MAGICIAN'S REVENGE

Shakespeare's last comedy *The Tempest* is set on a lonely island. Its hero is Prospero, a shipwrecked former Duke of Milan. An old man now, Prospero uses his magical powers to gain revenge on those who had seized his dukedom years before, and also to find a husband for his daughter Miranda. In the production of the play shown here, the part of Prospero is played by Vanessa Redgrave.

THE COMEDIES
as published in the First Folio

The Tempest
The Two Gentlemen of Verona
The Merry Wives of Windsor
Measure for Measure
The Comedy of Errors
Much Ado About Nothing
Love's Labours Lost
Midsummer Night's Dream
The Merchant of Venice
As You Like It
The Taming of the Shrew
All's Well that End's Well
Twelfth Night
The Winter's Tale

THE HISTORIES

RICHARD THE TIME-WASTER

One of Shakespeare's finest and most tragic history plays is *Richard II*, based on the life and reign of the king. Richard is a weak monarch who loses his throne to his cousin Henry Bolingbroke, who then becomes King Henry IV. Yet Shakespeare manages to turn Richard into a sympathetic character who comes to see the error of his ways.

THE HISTORIES
as published in the First Folio

King John
Richard II
Henry IV, part 1
Henry IV, part 2
Henry V
Henry VI, part 1
Henry VI, part 2
Henry VI, part 3
Richard III
Henry VIII

Although historians disagree on exactly when Shakespeare wrote his plays, much of his earlier work belongs in the category of 'histories'. He wrote two four-play cycles or tetralogies about kings of England who had reigned during the previous 200 years. The first featured three plays about Henry VI (1422–61) and a fourth about Richard III (1483–85). The second tetralogy featured one play about Richard II (1377–99), two about Henry IV (1399–1413) and one about Henry V (1413–22). For his information, Shakespeare drew on history books such as the *Chronicles of England, Scotlande and Irelande* by Raphael Holinshed, which was published in 1577. But he felt free to 'rearrange' the facts to make his plays exciting.

SHAKESPEARE'S LAST HISTORY PLAY

The last king that Shakespeare wrote about, maybe with John Fletcher, was Henry VIII (1509–47), the father of Queen Elizabeth I. Shakespeare is often thought to have been a keen supporter of the Tudor royal family, yet his portrait of Henry is not entirely flattering: '*This is the state of man,*' says Cardinal Wolsey in the play, '*He puts forth the tender leaves of hopes; tomorrow blossoms.../ The third day comes a frost, a killing frost...*'

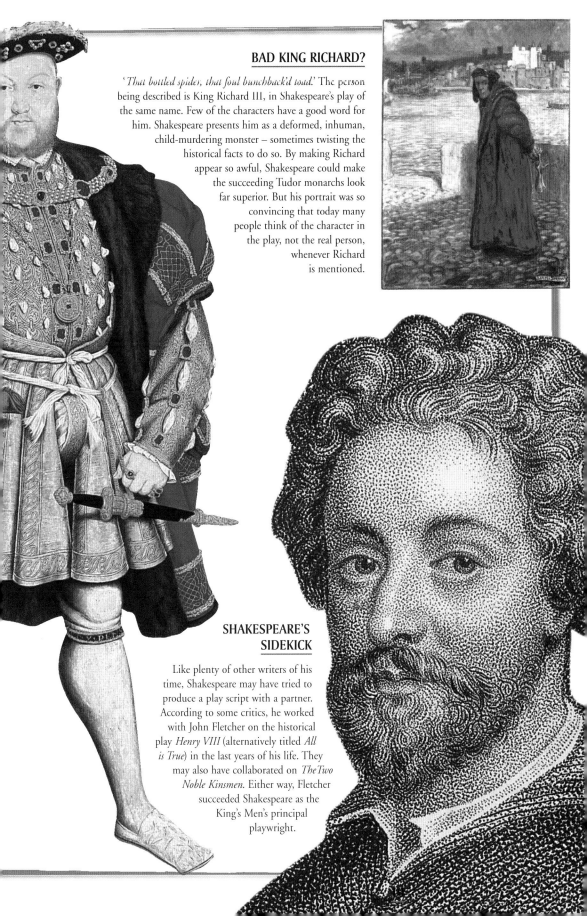

BAD KING RICHARD?

'*That bottled spider, that foul bunchback'd toad.*' The person being described is King Richard III, in Shakespeare's play of the same name. Few of the characters have a good word for him. Shakespeare presents him as a deformed, inhuman, child-murdering monster – sometimes twisting the historical facts to do so. By making Richard appear so awful, Shakespeare could make the succeeding Tudor monarchs look far superior. But his portrait was so convincing that today many people think of the character in the play, not the real person, whenever Richard is mentioned.

SHAKESPEARE'S SIDEKICK

Like plenty of other writers of his time, Shakespeare may have tried to produce a play script with a partner. According to some critics, he worked with John Fletcher on the historical play *Henry VIII* (alternatively titled *All is True*) in the last years of his life. They may also have collaborated on *The Two Noble Kinsmen*. Either way, Fletcher succeeded Shakespeare as the King's Men's principal playwright.

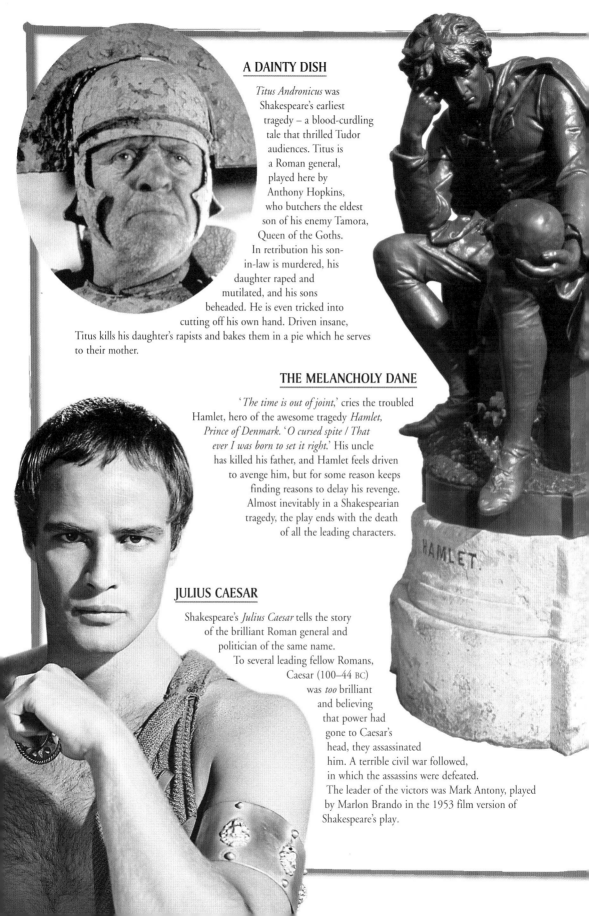

A DAINTY DISH

Titus Andronicus was
Shakespeare's earliest
tragedy – a blood-curdling
tale that thrilled Tudor
audiences. Titus is
a Roman general,
played here by
Anthony Hopkins,
who butchers the eldest
son of his enemy Tamora,
Queen of the Goths.
In retribution his son-
in-law is murdered, his
daughter raped and
mutilated, and his sons
beheaded. He is even tricked into
cutting off his own hand. Driven insane,
Titus kills his daughter's rapists and bakes them in a pie which he serves
to their mother.

THE MELANCHOLY DANE

'*The time is out of joint*,' cries the troubled
Hamlet, hero of the awesome tragedy *Hamlet,
Prince of Denmark*. '*O cursed spite / That
ever I was born to set it right*.' His uncle
has killed his father, and Hamlet feels driven
to avenge him, but for some reason keeps
finding reasons to delay his revenge.
Almost inevitably in a Shakespearian
tragedy, the play ends with the death
of all the leading characters.

JULIUS CAESAR

Shakespeare's *Julius Caesar* tells the story
of the brilliant Roman general and
politician of the same name.
To several leading fellow Romans,
Caesar (100–44 BC)
was *too* brilliant
and believing
that power had
gone to Caesar's
head, they assassinated
him. A terrible civil war followed,
in which the assassins were defeated.
The leader of the victors was Mark Antony, played
by Marlon Brando in the 1953 film version of
Shakespeare's play.

EARLY TRAGEDIES

*M*any people believe that the tragedies are his greatest achievements. The genres of comedy and tragedy go back to ancient Greek times. The Greek writer Aristotle said that tragedy was superior to comedy, because tragedies represent people as better than the norm, while comedies represent them as worse. Shakespeare's early tragedies are mainly set in past times, and usually involve an important person who suffers trials and tribulations before losing his life. Sometimes the plays' heroes are brought down by the workings of fate, or by their own fatal flaws, such as jealousy or pride. '*The fault lies not in our stars*,' as Julius Caesar remarks in the play of that name, '*but in ourselves*.'

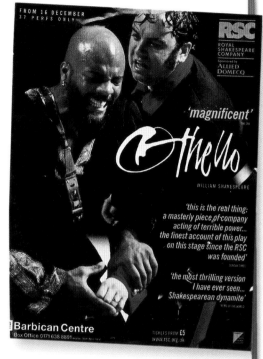

THE TORMENTS OF AN OUTSIDER

Othello, The Moor of Venice tells the tragic story of a black military hero who is not fully accepted by the white community in Venice, even though he has married the daughter of a leading senator. After an evil-minded whispering campaign by Iago, his own right-hand man, Othello wrongly believes that his wife Desdemona has been unfaithful to him. In a fit of jealousy, he kills her; then, when he finds he has been tricked, he kills himself too. This poster advertizes a production of *Othello* in which American actor Bob Wisdom played the lead.

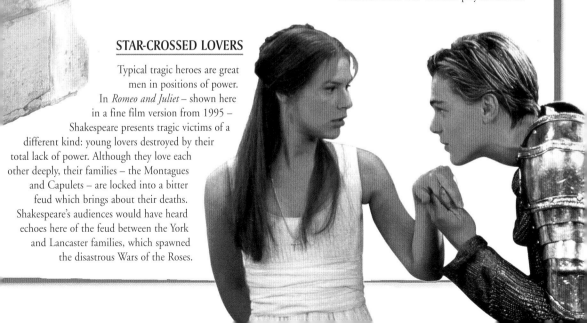

STAR-CROSSED LOVERS

Typical tragic heroes are great men in positions of power. In *Romeo and Juliet* – shown here in a fine film version from 1995 – Shakespeare presents tragic victims of a different kind: young lovers destroyed by their total lack of power. Although they love each other deeply, their families – the Montagues and Capulets – are locked into a bitter feud which brings about their deaths. Shakespeare's audiences would have heard echoes here of the feud between the York and Lancaster families, which spawned the disastrous Wars of the Roses.

HISTORICAL INSPIRATION

This book, Raphael Holinshed's popular *Chronicles* (first published in 1577) was a vital source for Shakespeare. It gave him information on actual historical figures, such as Macbeth, as well as mythical British monarchs, such as King Lear. He also discovered ancient rulers, such as the ancient Briton Cunobelin, whose name Shakespeare changed into Cymbeline. The *Chronicles* helped Tudor people, who looked to the past to understand the present, to forge a strong sense of national identity.

KINGS TO COME

Macbeth is Shakespeare's magnificent 'Scottish play'. Three witches meet two generals in the King of Scotland's army. To one, Macbeth, they predict that he will rise to be king. To the other, Banquo, they predict that his descendants will rule Scotland. This sets Macbeth, encouraged by his ambitious wife, on a blood-stained course to seizing the crown but finally losing his life. Interestingly, King James I claimed descent from Fleance, the son of Banquo.

THE TRAGEDIES
as published in the First Folio

Coriolanus
Titus Andronicus
Romeo and Juliet
Timon of Athens
Julius Caeser
Macbeth
Hamlet
King Lear
Othello
Antony and Cleopatra
Cymbeline, King of Britain

A MAN ALONE

Coriolanus is a tragedy about power politics in ancient Rome. Coriolanus becomes a kind of god by excelling at warfare. But his arrogance makes him think that he can live '*as if a man were author of himself, and knew no other kin*'. So when he dies, few have pity for him, since he has cut himself off from everyone.

LATER TRAGEDIES

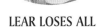

Some of Shakespeare's most moving tragedies were written in the last part of his career, as James I succeeded Elizabeth I to the English throne. This was the era of the Gunpowder Plot: tense, unsettled times when people feared a return to the kind of upheavals last seen 150 years before, during the Wars of the Roses. *Macbeth, King Lear* and *Antony and Cleopatra* all focus on what can go wrong inside a kingdom or empire if its rulers are not people of the highest calibre, with a true sense of duty and responsibility. Yet Shakespeare also seems to suggest that his heroes' lives can be shaped by forces far beyond their control: in *King Lear*, the Earl of Gloucester laments that the gods treat people as children treat flies – *'they kill us for their sport.'* Such themes give these tragedies an undying appeal, regardless of the circumstances in which they were written.

LEAR LOSES ALL

'*This feather stirs; she lives!*' the dying king cries over his beloved daughter Cordelia. '*If it be so,*
It is a chance which does
redeem all sorrows
That ever I have felt!'
But he is deceived; he has lost her, just as he has lost his kingdom – and all because he divided his kingdom and tried to abdicate his duties as the monarch of ancient Britain. This is a violent, pessimistic play, with little light relief.

A WOMAN OF INFINITE VARIETY

This is an advertisement for the 1963 film *Cleopatra*, based on Shakespeare's epic tragedy *Antony and Cleopatra*, which starred Elizabeth Taylor as the Queen of Ancient Egypt. The play charts the Queen's passionate love affair with Roman ruler Mark Antony, who also appears in Shakespeare's tragedy *Julius Caesar*. To triumph in a man's world he takes on many guises, from sexy seductress o wily politician, but finally she and her lover die defeated.

SONNETS & OTHER POEMS

THE PASSIONATE PILGRIM

Some of Shakespeare's early verse was published in a volume of 20 poems called *The Passionate Pilgrim* (1599). Some of the passion and frustration of love can be sensed in these lines:

'Crabbed age and youth cannot live together:

Youth is full of pleasance, age is full of care;

Youth like summer morn, age like winter weather;

Youth like summer brave, age like winter bare...

Age, I do abhor thee; youth, I do adore thee;

O! my love, my love is young!'

hakespeare was not just the greatest playwright England has ever produced, he was also one of its finest poets, especially on the subject of love. His first two long poems, *Venus and Adonis* (1593) and *The Rape of Lucrece* (*c*.1594) were dedicated to his young patron and friend Henry Wriothesley (1573–1624), third Earl of Southampton. Shakespeare may have worked on both poems outside London, for during the period 1592–94 plague struck the capital. All theatrical performances were suspended, and those who were able to, left the city. In 1609 Shakespeare's *Sonnets* (short, 14-line poems) were published. Their themes are love and betrayal, and feature a '*fair youth*' (who could be Wriothesley or the Earl of Pembroke) and a '*dark lady*'. In the *Sonnets* Shakespeare expresses every shade of passion with such genius that the collection has been called Shakespeare's own '*spiritual biography*'.

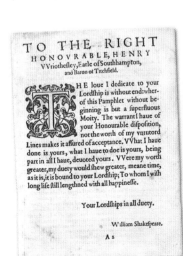

DEDICATED TO A PATRON

Like all authors at the time, Shakespeare needed a patron. He looked to the Earl of Southampton for patronage by dedicating his first published work, *Venus and Adonis,* to him. He was successful, and the dedication in his second work, *The Rape of Lucrece* (*left*), shows Shakespeare's gratitude. *The Rape of Lucrece* was a more sombre and much longer work. Inspired, like *Venus,* by a tale from Ovid's *Metamorphoses,* the poem helped to secure Shakespeare's reputation as an outstanding poet of love.

SHAKESPEARE IN LOVE?

In 1601, Shakespeare's mysterious poem *The Phoenix and Turtle* appeared in a verse collection that celebrated the love of Sir John Salisbury for his wife Ursula, the daughter of the Earl of Derby. It has been suggested that the turtle-dove in the poem stands for Shakespeare himself, and the phoenix a nun, now dead, whom he had once loved. Below is the poignant funeral song from the poem.

THE PHOENIX & TURTLE

Beauty, truth, and rarity,
Grace in all simplicity,
Here enclosed in cinders lie.

Death is now the phoenix nest;
And the tutrle's loyal breast
To eternity doth rest,

Leaving no posterity:—
'Twas not their infirmity,
It was married chastity.

Truth may seem, but cannot be;
Beauty brag, but 'tis not she;
Truth and beauty buried be.

To this urn let those repair
That are either true or fair;
For these dead birds sigh a prayer.

A BEAUTEOUS ROSE

In Shakespeare's published collection of 154 *Sonnets* (1609), one of the best-loved and most-quoted is Sonnet 54, which begins:

'*O! how much more doth beauty beauteous seem*

By that sweet ornament which truth doth give:

The rose looks fair, but fairer we it deem

For that sweet odour which doth in it live.'

VENUS & ADONIS

This plate illustrated a later edition of the first of all Shakespeare's works to be published: *Venus and Adonis*. This was a mythological poem published in 1593, based on a tale in the *Metamorphoses* by the ancient Roman poet Ovid. Before 1640, no fewer than 16 editions of the poem were printed, as so many people wanted to read it. No other work by Shakespeare had so many printings during this period.

MODERN TAKES ON 'THE MOOR'

Shakespeare's *Othello* has been adapted in several different musical ways. *All Night Long*, a British film made in 1961, set the story in the world of jazz. *Catch My Soul*, shown here, was a theatrical rock-opera version of the play, filmed in 1974, with musicians Bonnie and Delaney Bramlett using as much Shakespearean poetry as they could fit into their songs.

OPERATIC OTHELLO

The compelling, emotional themes of Shakespeare's plays make them especially suitable for operatic treatment. The Frenchmen Charles Gounod and Ambroise Thomas composed operas about Romeo and Juliet (1867) and Hamlet (1868); while between 1847 and 1893 the Italian Guiseppe Verdi based operas on *Macbeth*, *Othello* and *The Merry Wives of Windsor*. Above is a modern production of the second of these plays, with Dame Kiri Te Kanawa singing the role of Othello's wife, Desdemona.

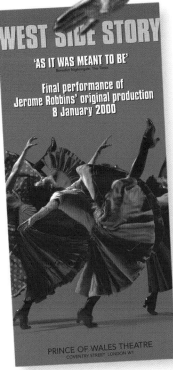

WEST SIDE STORY

'AS IT WAS MEANT TO BE'
Benedict Nightingale, The Times

Final performance of
Jerome Robbins' original production
8 January 2000

PRINCE OF WALES THEATRE
COVENTRY STREET, LONDON W1

MEAN-STREETS MAKEOVER

The musical play *West Side Story*, with a score by Leonard Bernstein and lyrics by Stephen Sondheim, was first produced in 1957. The play, situated in New York, was based on Shakespeare's *Romeo and Juliet*. The feuding of the Montagues and Capulets was replaced by modern-day New York street violence between white and Puerto Rican gangs. An instant success, it featured some dazzling choreography and was made into a film in 1961. Songs from the musical, such as 'Maria' and 'Somewhere' have been covered by many artists ranging from the growling pop genius Tom Waits to the great opera star Jose Carreras.

MUSIC & DANCE

In Shakespeare's time, only a few trumpet blasts would accompany the action in a theatre. Europe's great composers later made up for that by penning many pieces inspired by Shakespeare's work. The Germans Brahms and Schubert wrote music for songs from the plays, the Hungarian composer Liszt composed a symphonic poem on *Hamlet*, while the Russian Tchaikovsky and Italian Verdi produced wonderful music for Shakespearean ballet and opera. Possibly the most famous piece composed for a Shakespeare performance came in Felix Mendelssohn's incidental music for *A Midsummer Night's Dream*. 'The Wedding March' is played at many marriage ceremonies today. The rock and pop world has been affected by Shakespeare too. Dire Straits had a hit single in 1981 with *Romeo and Juliet*, while the 1995 film *William Shakespeare's Romeo & Juliet* had a best-selling soundtrack which included songs by Radiohead, the Cardigans and Garbage.

SHREWD ADAPTATION

Kiss Me Kate opened in New York at the end of 1948 and became the fourth longest-running musical with 1,077 shows. It has often been revived since, and in 1953 it was filmed. Its plot weaves Shakespeare's comedy *The Taming of the Shrew* into a parallel story of modern-day domestic strife. There is a classic Cole Porter score to enjoy, featuring the songs 'Too Darn Hot' and 'So in Love'.

SHAKESPEARE IN RUSSIA

In the 19th century, Shakespeare provided the inspiration for a variety of Russian creative geniuses. The Russian poet, Pushkin, praised and imitated him. The Russian playwright, Ostrovsky, adapted and translated his work. Characters in the novels of the famous Russian writer, Dostoevsky, quoted and discussed him at length. And his plays stirred the celebrated Russian composer Tchaikovsky into writing symphonic fantasies, overtures and incidental music. Here a Russian ballet company is performing to music he wrote for Shakespeare's *Romeo and Juliet*.

THE WRITER'S INFLUENCE

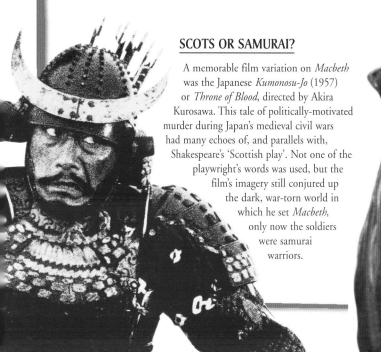

INTERNATIONAL *HAMLET*

Hamlet has proved to be one of Shakespeare's more adaptable plays, thanks to its universal themes. In 1955, an Indian version was filmed in Bombay, and ten years later the story was relocated in northern Ghana for a fascinating stage and film interpretation entitled *Hamile*. This picture shows a scene from an unusual modern-age Finnish movie, *Hamlet Goes Business* (1987).

$\mathcal{S}$hakespeare died almost 400 years ago, but he has left the world a great legacy. All over the world, new and exciting performances of his plays are staged each year. Meanwhile, his work continues to be filmed in a bewildering variety of forms and languages. His work survives because he always kept in mind what his audiences – educated and uneducated alike – might want to see and hear. But he has also inspired many other playwrights, as well as artists, musicians, poets and novelists, to put their own spin on his stories or characters.

Some of this new work has been equally inspired; sometimes it has seemed to be taking huge liberties with his 'sacred' texts. Yet Shakespeare himself drew heavily on the work of others. He would probably have been fascinated to see how later generations have drawn on his own pieces.

SCOTS OR SAMURAI?

A memorable film variation on *Macbeth* was the Japanese *Kumonosu-Jo* (1957) or *Throne of Blood*, directed by Akira Kurosawa. This tale of politically-motivated murder during Japan's medieval civil wars had many echoes of, and parallels with, Shakespeare's 'Scottish play'. Not one of the playwright's words was used, but the film's imagery still conjured up the dark, war-torn world in which he set *Macbeth*, only now the soldiers were samurai warriors.

PETER GREENAWAY PROSPEROS BÜCHER NACH WILLIAM SHAKESPEARES DER STURM

TEMPESTUOUS TREATMENTS

Shakespeare's late play *The Tempest* inspired two controversial film treatments by British directors: Derek Jarman's *The Tempest: by William Shakespeare, as Seen Through the Eyes of Derek Jarman* (1980), and *Prospero's Books* by Peter Greenaway (1991), a poster for which is shown here. Both films improvised around Shakespeare's original plot, with some scenes causing outrage and offence, but *Prospero's Books* did star one of the greatest actors ever to play Prospero on stage – Sir John Gielgud.

THE WOMAN IN THE WATER

One of many great painters to be inspired by Shakespeare was John Everett Millais (1829–96). This painting from 1852 shows Ophelia, an ill-fated character in *Hamlet* who drowns herself. The model who sat for the painting was ill-fated too. Lying in a bath heated from beneath by lamps, she caught such a severe cold when the lamps went out that her father threatened to sue the artist until he agreed to pay her doctor's bills!

MINOR BECOMES MAJOR

Rosencrantz and Guildenstern are two unimportant courtiers in Shakespeare's tragedy *Hamlet*. But the British playwright Tom Stoppard saw fresh dramatic possibilities in presenting the plot from their point of view, and wrote a whole new play about them: *Rosencrantz and Guildenstern Are Dead.* Here they are portrayed by Tim Roth and Gary Oldman in a film version from 1990, directed by Stoppard himself. '*A bit of Shakespeare, a bit of me, a bit more of that, off with me, on with Shakespeare,*' was how Stoppard described his work.

CELLULOID HEROES

One of the first black actors to play the lead in *Othello* on film was Laurence Fishburne, shown here in the 1995 movie. Alongside him is the villain Iago, played by the British stage and screen actor Kenneth Branagh. In 1996, Branagh also directed and starred in an epic 242-minute-long film version of *Hamlet* (the second-longest English-language film ever made). Branagh had already distinguished himself with *Henry V* (1989) and *Much Ado About Nothing* (1993).

GANGSTERS IN ANCIENT GREECE

In 1935 German director Max Reinhardt made a trail-blazing Hollywood film version of *A Midsummer Night's Dream*, a play set in old Athens. The parts were not played by classical actors but by major American film stars much better known for their modern-day roles as gangsters and glamour queens. James Cagney, Mickey Rooney and Olivia de Havilland put on a great show, proving that Shakespeare's spellbinding words could sound good in any accent.

ALL THE WORLD'S A STAGE

In Shakespeare's time, the Globe Theatre on Bankside carried a Latine motto that in English means: '*All the World's a Stage.*' Today the whole world could be called a stage for the continuing presentation of the great playwright's works, whether on film or in theatres. Many people's view of English history comes, rightly or wrongly, from Shakespeare's writing. Furthermore, anyone who uses a phrase like '*the milk of human kindness*', '*the winter of our discontent*', '*To be or not to be*', '*O, brave new world*', or even '*My horse, my horse, my kingdom for a horse*' is quoting – possibly without knowing – from Shakespeare. His vocabulary was made up of over 21,000 words – including hundreds that he coined himself – and is probably the richest in the whole body of English literature. The magical way in which those words were woven together will ensure that, as long as the world has ears, he will be heard.

IN GOOD COMPANY

All the world may well be a stage, but many of the world's play-goers now flock to watch Shakespeare's work being staged at the Royal Shakespeare Theatre in Stratford-upon-Avon (*above*). This is one of the five home theatres of the Royal Shakespeare Company (R.S.C.), which also takes productions on tour around the UK, and also – in recent times – as far afield as the United States, Korea, Australia and India.

A HEAD FOR HUMOUR

'*Alas! poor Yorick, I knew him, Horatio; a fellow of infinite jest, of most excellent fancy...*' Laurence Olivier speaks some often-quoted lines from *Hamlet* in his English film version of the play, made in 1948. Yorick, whose skull the Prince of Denmark is holding, had been a court jester. The skull has figured in countless comedy sketches over the years, as well as in TV commercials.

PRINCESS OF DENMARK

Few stage actresses have thrilled audiences as much as the Frenchwoman Sarah Bernhardt (1844–1923). Around the turn of the 20th century she even won acclaim by taking the leading role in *Hamlet, Prince of Denmark*, although audiences found it harder to accept 'The Divine Sarah' playing the other Shakespearean parts of Macbeth and Othello. She is shown here posing as Hamlet in a brief film version in 1900. This was shown to the accompaniment of phonograph records relaying the music and voices.

DID YOU KNOW?

That Shakespeare's grave marker did not always show him holding his quill? Shakespeare was originally portrayed with a bag of grain in his hand, but the people of Stratford decided to replace it with a quill in order to draw in more tourists.

That Shakespeare married an Avon lady? Shakespeare was only 18 when he married Anne Hathaway, who was 26 years old. She was already three months pregnant with their first child, Susanna, so the couple had to get a special license from the Bishop, allowing them to marry outside the parish in which they lived.

That some people believe that Shakespeare did not write his works at all? Doubters believe that he could not have written such intelligent pieces as he did not attend university, nor was he widely travelled. There have been several suggestions as to who wrote the masterpieces, including Edward de Vere, the 17th Earl of Oxford, Christopher Marlowe, Daniel Defoe; even Queen Elizabeth I! However, Francis Bacon has been tipped the firm favourite!

That Shakespeare used his plays to insult people? *'That which we call a rose by any other name would smell as sweet...'* This line, from Romeo and Juliet, was a sneaky insult towards the Rose Theatre in London, a direct competitor of the Globe Theatre, for which Shakespeare wrote plays. The Rose Theatre was renowned for smelling terrible, as there was an open toilet area right behind it!

That Shakespeare was a man of quite a few words? Shakespeare's works contain an approximate total of 29,066 words, many of which were his own creations. There were no dictionaries available to Shakespeare and his contemporaries, as the first was not compiled until 1606. The average person today has a vocabulary of roughly 45,000 words.

That poor members of Shakespeare's audience were known as 'groundlings'? This is because they were forced to stand on the ground in front of the stage, in the cheapest part of the theatre! The ceiling of Shakespeare's stages was known as 'The Heavens'.

ACKNOWLEDGEMENTS

We would like to thank: Graham Rich and Elizabeth Wiggans for their assistance and David Hobbs for his map of the world.
Copyright © 2003 *ticktock* Entertainment Ltd,
Unit 2, Orchard Business Centre, North Farm Road, Tunbridge Wells, Kent, TN2 3XF, U.K. First published in Great Britain 1998.
All rights reserved. No part of this publication may be reproduced, stored in a retrieval system, or transmitted in any form or by any means electronic, mechanical, photocopying, recording or otherwise, without prior written permission of the copyright owner.
A CIP catalogue record for this book is available from the British Library. ISBN 1 86007 409 X
Picture research by Image Select. Printed in Egypt.

Picture Credits: t=top, b=bottom, c=centre, l=left, r=right, OFC=outside front cover, OBC=outside back cover, IFC=inside front cover

AKG; OBC, 7tl, 24/25c; Art Archive: 2/3c, 8c, 12c, 12bl, 12/13c, 14tl, 17tl, 17br, 22l; Board of Trustees of the National Museums and Galleries on Merseyside (Walker Art Gallery, Liverpool); 18/19c; Bodleian Library; 24bl; British Library; 5tr, 6bl, 22tr; Corbis; OFC, OFC, 3tl, 3br, 6tl, 13tr, 15tl, 20/21tc; David Hobbs; 4tl, 10/11 main pic, 11tc, 12tr; Devonshire House, Chatsworth; 7c; Kobal Collection; 15b, 20tl, 30c, 30/31c; Mary Evans Picture Library; OFC, OFC, 2tl, 2br, 4bl, 4/5c, 5br, 6/7c, 8tl, 18tl, 19br; MovieGoods Inc; 26tr; Photobank; 9tr, 31tr; Pictor; 9bl; Public Record Office; 13br; Ronald Grant Archive; 20br, 21tr, 21br, 23br, 26bc, 26cl, 26/7c, 27tr, 27br, 28tl, 28bl, 29tl, 29b, 30tl, 31bc; Shakespeare's Birthplace; 9br; Shakespeare's Globe; 16/17c; Tate Picture Gallery; 29tr.

The following pictures are reproduced, courtesy of the Windsor Shakespeare Collection;
OFC, 8tr, 14bl, 15tr, 16tl, 16tl, 17cl, 19tr, 22/23c, 23tr, 24tl, 25tr

Every effort has been made to trace the copyright holders and we apologize in advance for any unintentional omissions.
We would be pleased to insert the appropriate acknowledgement in any subsequent edition of this publication.

snapping-turtle
guide